The CHURCH Graphically Presented

"Study to shew thyself approved unto God, a workman that needeth not to be ashamed, rightly dividing the word of truth."

2 Timothy 2:15

Cover and Illustration: Leonardo Costa

ISBN: 978-1-945774-36-2

Dispensational Publishing House, Inc.
PO Box 3181
Taos, NM 87571

www.DispensationalPublishing.com

Ordering Information:
Quantity or wholesale discounts are available for churches, associations, and retailers. For details, contact the publisher.

2 3 4 5 6 7 8 9 10 1

CONTENTS

PART 3: THE PRACTICE OF THE CHURCH

From the Author

For most Christians, the church plays the most important organizational role of our lives. Outside of our own family, the church is the organization that most affects our thinking, our worldview, and our social life, and our emotional, spiritual, and even physical well-being. Many of us are part of a church "from the cradle to the grave."

In spite of the church's influence, however, many of us have become surprised at how broad the range of church-theology (ecclesiology) really is. From Catholicism to Protestantism to Evangelicalism to Fundamentalism and all sorts of other -isms, the doctrine of the church is far from settled.

The charts in this book are designed to help the student work through his or her ecclesiology and help shape a Biblical doctrine of the church. The book should be approached with an open Bible and a mind closed to anything outside the clear teaching of the Bible. Set aside the denominational propaganda and the evangelical mantra and see what the Bible actually teaches (or does not teach) about this thing we call church.

As you study, be sure to *rightly divide* so that you do not *wrongly apply* Scripture to the church when it is not about the church! And, as you learn, be prepared to *question the assumptions* you have picked up along the way. You may find that so many things that were presented as "the gospel truth" are not *truth* at all…let alone *gospel.*

In His Grace;

Randy White,
Taos, NM

THE BIBLICAL NATURE OF THE CHURCH

The **CHURCH** *Graphically Presented*

THE FALL OF ISRAEL AND THE RISE OF THE CHURCH

The Key Transition for Accurate Theology

ASSEMBLY OF JEWISH BELIEVERS

33-44 A.D.

Led by Peter

- Watching, 1:1-11
- Waiting, 1:12-26
- Witnessing, 2:1-47

Acts 3-4

Growth: Persecution, Partnership, Proclamation

- Internal Threat 5:1-16
- External Threat 5:17-42
- Internal Threat 6:1-7
- External Threat 6:8-8:3
- Divided but not conquered 8:4-11:30
- The end of the Jerusalem Era 12:1-25

THE CHURCH-AGE ASSEMBLY

44-66 AD

Assembly of Jewish Believers led by James
Gentile Assembly led by Paul

1st Missionary Journey 13:1-15:35	46-50 AD
2nd Missionary Journey 15:36-18:22	50-52 AD
3rd Missionary Journey 18:23-21:16	52-57 AD
Imprisoned in Jerusalem: 21:17-23:35	57 AD
Imprisoned in Caesarea 24-26	57-59 AD
Imprisoned in Rome 27-28	59-66 AD

Notes

BIBLICAL COVENANTS

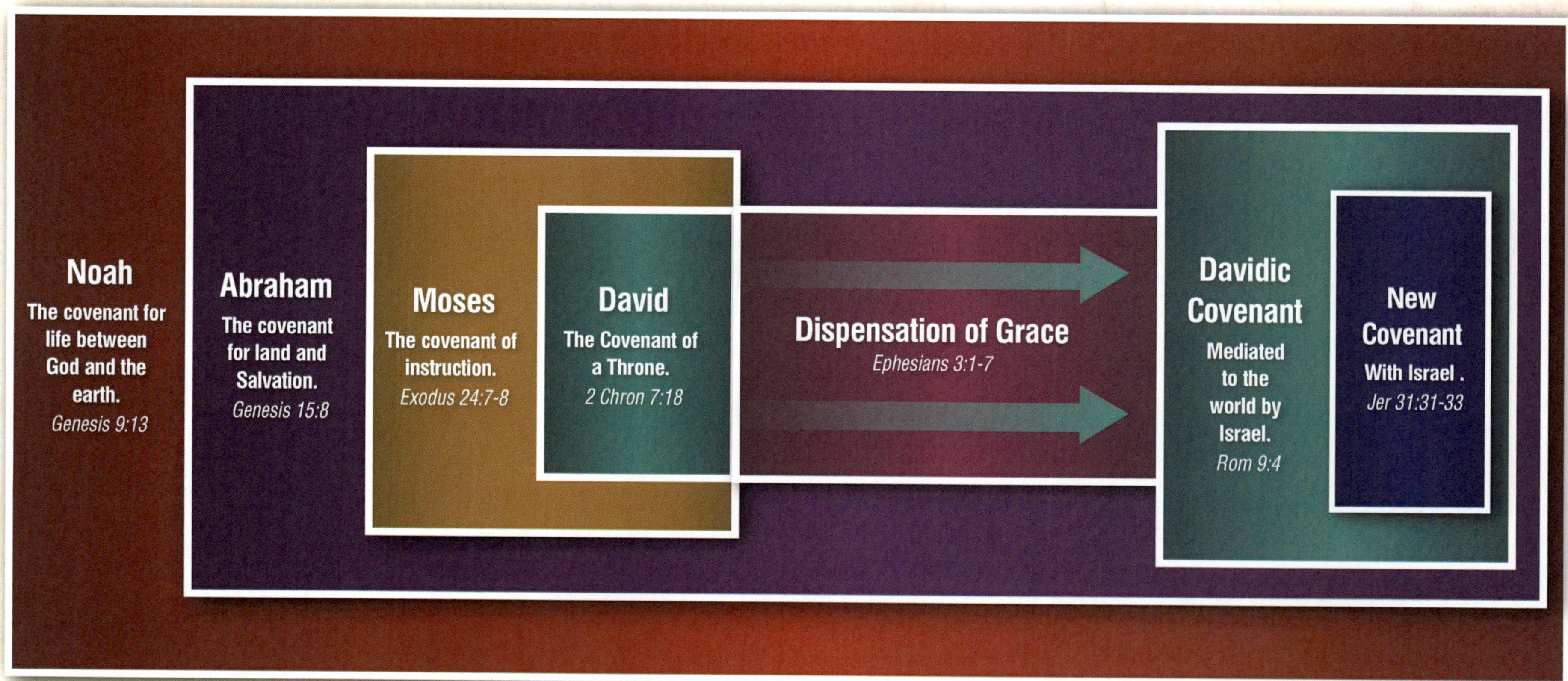

Notes

PAUL AND THE 12 APOSTLES

TWELVE APOSTLES

The 12 were sent to proclaim the gospel of the Kingdom, a message of repentance - Acts 2:38-40

The 12 were under the leadership of Peter - Matthew 16:19

The 12 would have 12 thrones, judging Israel - Matt 19:28

The 12 were to preach Christ as the Messiah, coming to judge Israel and rule over the nations - Acts 3:19-21

The 12 were sent to teach obedience to the Law for Israel - Matthew 28:19-20, Acts 21:19-20

PAUL

Paul's salvation and training was outside of all influence of the 12 - Galatians 1:11-12

Paul was the recipient of a mystery revelation, not a prophetic revelation - Ephesians 3:2-3

Paul magnified his ministry over that of the 12 - Romans 11:13

Paul gave no deference to the 12 – Galatians 2:6

Notes

THE PROPHETIC PLAN

Notes

THE MYSTERY REVEALED

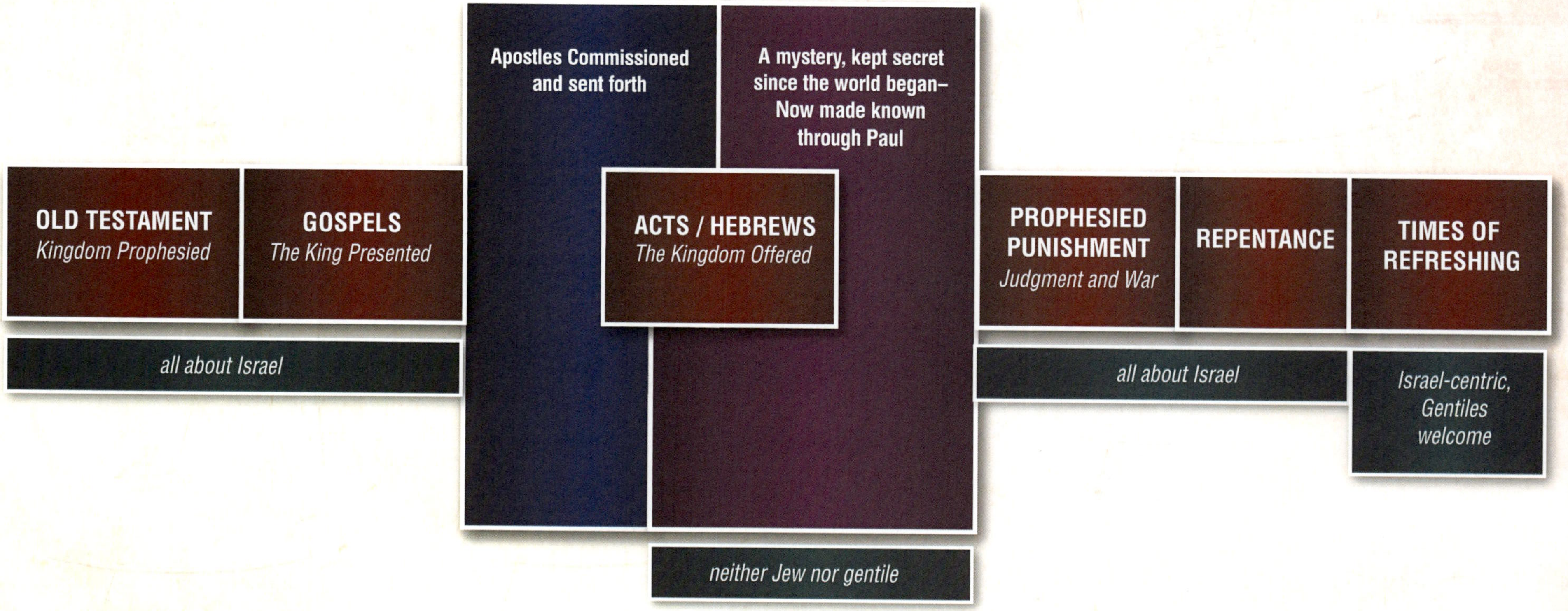

Notes

THE GOSPEL OF THE KINGDOM AND THE GOSPEL OF GRACE

THE GOSPEL OF THE KINGDOM	THE GOSPEL OF GRACE
John came "preaching the baptism of repentance for the forgivenenss of sins" (Luke 3:3)	Believe and you will be saved (Acts 16:31)
A requirement of "fruits worthy of repentance" (Luke 3:8)	God is faithful even if we are not (2 Tim. 2:13)
A requirement of personal righteousness (Luke 3:10-14)	A gift of imputed righteousness (2 Cor. 5:19-21)

Notes

WHAT KIND OF ECCLESIA IS THERE?

THE ECCLESIA OF THE WILDERNESS	THE ECCLESIA WHICH JESUS WOULD BUILD	THE ECCLESIA OF PETER	THE ECCLESIA OF PAUL	THE ECCLESIA OF ALL BELIEVERS AT THE RAPTURE
Acts 7:38	Matthew 16:18	Luke 12:32, John 21:15	1 Timothy 1:15-16, 2 Corinthians 11:28	1 Thessalonians 4:16-17
The Septuagint used the word *Ecclesia* 54 times, showing that it was a well-used, non-Christian word at the time of Jesus.	The ecclesia of the Age of the Church is built on the faith of the completed work of Jesus, not on the identity of Jesus as "the Christ."	Peter's ecclesia began at Pentecost and proclaimed "Repent and Be Baptized" to prepare for the arrival of the Kingdom.	Paul was the first member and the prototype of the ecclesia of free-grace believers.	The rapture of the ecclesia is the resurrection and rapture of the entirety of the Ecclesia of Paul throughout history.
Assembled at the Tabernacle	Assembles at the Judgment seat and Jerusalem	Assembled at the Temple, synagogues, and house-to-house	Assembled in local congregations	Assembles in the air, with the Lord
Organization: National	Organization: Theocracy	Organization: Apostolic	Organization: Independent	Organization: Heavenly
Earthly leader: Moses	Earthly leader: Jesus	Eartlhy leader: Peter	Earthly leader: Paul	Earthly leader: none
If we make each ecclesia to be "the church" then we abandon dispensational theology for covenant theology.				

Notes

THE HISTORY OF THE CHURCH

THE DEVELOPMENT OF THE ACTS 2 CONCEPT

THE ACTS 2 CONCEPT IS THE IDEA THAT THE CHURCH WAS BIRTHED AT PENTECOST		
This concept is taught without question by all forms of Christianity today	To question this assumption is considered heretical in almost all forms of Christianity today	It is doubtful that there is any such teaching prior to the development of the Nicene Creed, which teaches "one Holy Catholic and Apostolic" church
The Acts 2 Concept is a Catholic doctrine which was never questioned by those who followed		
Scripture does not denote a beginning of "the church age" nor of the church as an organization		

Notes

THE UNIVERSAL CHURCH

A UNIVERSALITY OF ACCEPTANCE	A SLOW DEVELOPMENT IN HISTORY
"The universal church is made up of all believers in Jesus Christ worldwide." -GotQuestions	Prior to 4th Century, the doctrine was unheard of
	4th - 16th Century - the doctrine was Catholic vs "Baptist"
	16th Century to Present - only fundamentalists reject the doctrine

Notes

A HISTORY OF THE BRIDE OF CHRIST THEOLOGY

A HISTORY OF THE BRIDE OF CHRIST THEOLOGY			
Tertullian (3rd Century) appears to be the first to make mention of the church as a bride, saying, "By the mouth of Isaiah He also says exultingly of the Father: 'Let my soul rejoice in the Lord; for He hath clothed me with the garment of salvation and with the tunic of joy, as a bridegroom. He hath put a mitre round about my head, as a bride.' To Himself likewise He appropriates the church, concerning which the same Spirit says to Him: 'Thou shalt clothe Thee with them all, as with a bridal ornament.' This spouse Christ invites home to Himself"	Cyprian (3rd Century) clearly said, "He is the Bridegroom, having the Church as His bride, from whom children should be spiritually born."	For the first two centuries there is no mention nor teaching of the church as the Bride of Christ	Through most of church history, the bride concept was a mystical union between a virgin (i.e.: nun) and the Lord

Notes

THE BRIDE OF CHRIST: AN OLD TESTAMENT OVERVIEW

AN OLD TESTAMENT OVERVIEW

<table>
<tr><th>Old Testament use of Bride</th><th>Old Testament use of "Beulah"</th><th>Conclusion of the Old Testament</th></tr>
<tr><td>Isaiah 49:18 - the first use of the word bride is used of Israel (in an illustrative sense)</td><td rowspan="2">Isaiah 62:4 - the Land will be called "married."</td><td rowspan="3">The Old Testament uses illustrations of the bride, and is always in relation to Israel</td></tr>
<tr><td>Isaiah 61:10 - the second use of the word bride is used of Israel (in an illustrative sense)</td></tr>
<tr><td>Isaiah 62:5 - God will rejoice over Israel as the bridgroom rejoiceth over the bride.</td><td rowspan="2">Jeremiah 3:14 - God says to Israel, I am married to you</td></tr>
<tr><td>Jeremiah 2:32 - Israel is chastized because a bride does not forget her attire, yet she has forgotten God.</td><td rowspan="3">The Old Testament is explicit in the use of marriage, to Israel alone</td></tr>
<tr><td>Jeremiah 7:34 - A prophecy that the voice of the bride will be silent and the land shall be desolate. See also Jeremiah 16:9 and 25:10</td><td rowspan="2">Malachi 2:11 - God is upset that Judah married the daughter of a strange god</td></tr>
<tr><td>Jeremiah 33:11 - the previous prophecies of desolation and silence come to an end when God will cause to return the captivity of the land</td></tr>
</table>

Notes

THE BRIDE OF CHRIST: A NEW TESTAMENT OVERVIEW

A NEW TESTAMENT OVERVIEW

THE GOSPELS		THE REVELATION		THE APOSTLE PAUL	
John 3:39	The bridegroom is defined as Jesus. Could anyone legitimately assume the bride is different than in all the other Scriptures of John's dispensation?	Revelation 19:7	There are numerous references to the Kingdom of God as a wedding feast (Matt 22:2, 25:1, etc). Revelation 22 identifies the bride. Further, the church does not "make herself ready," but is made ready by grace through faith	Ephesians 5:24-27	A husband is to have a sacrificial love as Christ loved the church. Taken definitively but used illustratively
		Revelation 21:2	John saw New Jerusalem "prepared as a bride." This non-definitive description is of the same level as the Ephesians passages used to "definitively" declare the church as the bride	Ephesians 5:32	The church is mysteriously, as body of Christ, "one flesh" just as a husband and wife
		Revelation 21:9-10	A definitive yet ignored declaration	2 Corinthians 11:2	Illustration of dedication, proving no conclusion beyond its illustration
		Revelation 22:17	To read this as "the church" after the context of the previous chapter is irresponsible		

Notes

THE BRIDE OF CHRIST: WHY IT MATTERS

WHAT DOES IT MATTER?		
It causes the church to see herself as something she is not and thus miss seeing herself as what she actually is	Seeing herself as something she is not, she begins to express herself as something she is not	It is a form of replacement theology

Notes

THE MARK OF TRUE CHURCHES

THREE DISTINCT TRUTHS			THREE DISTINCT PRIORITIES		
The Bible alone as the authority for faith and practice	The accountability of man to God alone for Spiritual righteousness	The ability of every man to interpret the Bible fully and correctly on his own	Autonomy of the local church in its government	A regenerate church membership	Local control of ordination and ordinances

Notes

WHAT MAKES A CHURCH?

BELIEVERS	MEMBERSHIP	ORGANIZATION
A church is unique among organizations and networks in that it is composed of those who have placed their faith in Jesus Christ for salvation.	To be considered a church, the group of believers must have some membership criteria and standard, regardless of how formal or informal.	The membership must determine the organizational and governmental function of the church.
The church with believers in membership together and with an organizational structure is "local" regardless of the location of the members.		

Notes

THREE STRANDS OF CHURCH DOCTRINE (IN THEOLOGY)

	CATHOLIC	PROTESTANT	FUNDAMENTALIST
CONSTITUTION	The church is all baptized members	The church is all baptized, dead or alive	The church is believers who have joined in membership
POWER	The church is the Kingdom and exercises dominion	This church (not that one) is the Kingdom and exercises dominion	The church is a family of faith and the family exercises dominion, but only in the home
ISRAEL	Israel is the Old Testament church, replaced by the New Testament church	Retained the Catholic idea of Israel	Israel is distinct from the church and has a past and future role in the plan of God
SALVATION	Salvation is freely sought and is given by the church	Salvation is by election and is given by divine sovereignty	Salvation is freely sought and is given by grace through faith
THE BIBLE	Contains the word of God, but Jesus is the Word of God	Is the ultimate rule, but requires creeds, confessions, and synods	Is inerrant and infallible and can be interpreted without creeds, confessions, synods, or church
COVENANTS	Is living under the New Covenant	Is living under the New Covenant	Is not under a covenant of any kind
ESCHATOLOGY	Amillennial	Amillennial or Postmillennial	Pre-Tribulational and Premillennial
POLITY	Episcopal (rule by Bishops)	Presbyterian (rule by Elders)	Congregational (rule by membership)

Notes

THREE STRANDS OF CHURCH DOCTRINE (IN DENOMINATIONS) – PART 1

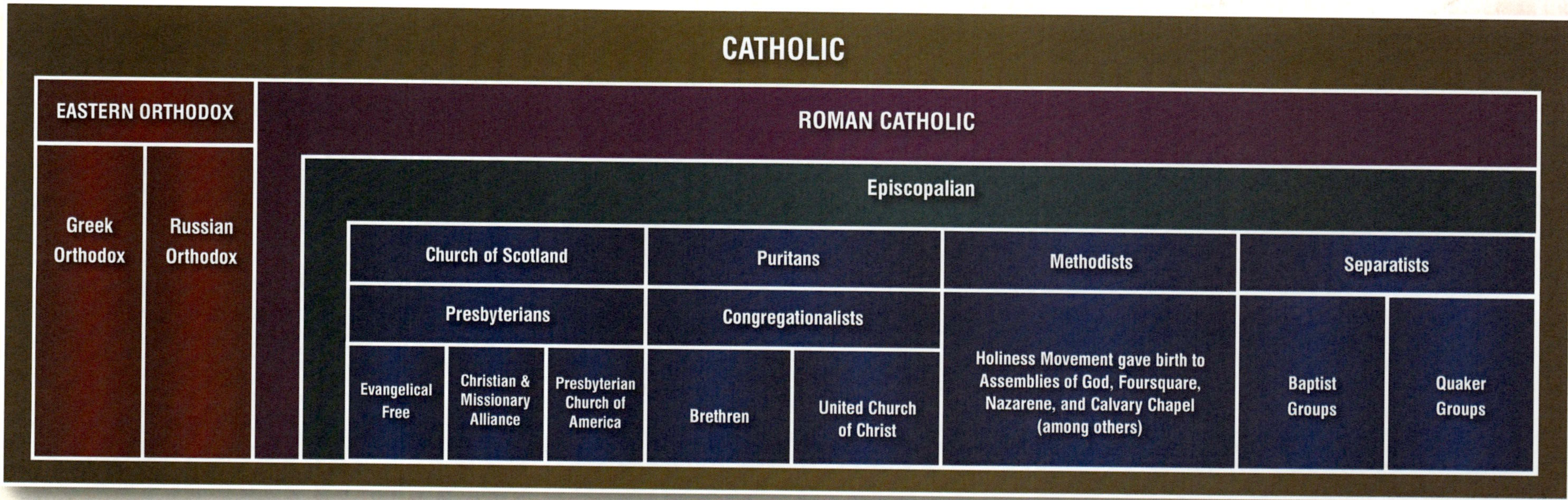

Notes

THREE STRANDS OF CHURCH DOCTRINE (IN DENOMINATIONS) – PART 2

PROTESTANT			FUNDAMENTALIST	
Lutheran	Reformed		Many of the fundamentalist groups came from Anabaptists, Waldensians, and other pre-reformation reformers. Other early fundamentalists broke off Protestant or Episcopalian groups. Today, the majority of fundamentalists are Baptist in ecclesiology and heritage	Evangelical churches shifted away from the fundamentalists toward increasing ecumenicalism and pragmatism. Most evangelicals are Baptist or non-denominational
Lutheranism has splintered into numerous denominations based on location and ideology	German Reformed (Reformed Church in the USA)	Dutch Reformed (Reformed Church of America)		

Notes

THE PRACTICE OF THE CHURCH

FREEDOM IN CHRIST

"Having forgiven you of all your trespasses"
Col. 2:13

"Blotting out the handwriting of ordinances that was against us."
Col. 2:14

"Having spoiled principalities and powers"
Col. 2:15

"let no man therefore judge you" Col. 2:16

Notes

THE VOICE OF GOD FOR BELIEVERS TODAY

THE VOICE OF GOD FOR BELIEVERS TODAY*			
The voice of the Evangelical Industrial Complex is the Voice of God for Denominations	The voice of the denomination is the voice of God for the pastors	The voice of the pastor and local church is the voice of God for the church member	The voice of the church member is the voice of God for the lost
The Bible is the Word of God and is scarcely known, taught, or used as a foundation			

*Adapted from Central Baptist Seminary Quarterly, Vol. 4, No. 2, Pg 3, 1961.

Notes

DOES THE CHURCH HAVE ORDINANCES?

THE UNIVERSALITY	THE BIBLE SPEAKS	THE NECESSARY CONCLUSION
Practically without exception, baptism and the Lord's Supper are accepted as ordinances in all Protestant, evangelical, charismatic, and fundamentalist churches, both denominational and non-denominational	Baptism: Matthew 28:19 The Lord's Supper: Luke 22:19 Footwashing: John 13:14 Other: Luke 6:27 (and many others)	The "ordinances" were hand-selected, cafeterial style, from among various commands given by the Lord to the Apostles. Our Lord never gave an ordinance to the church, which was a mystery at the time of His ministry

SHOULD A CHURCH PRACTICE ORDINANCES?

To teach them as "ordained" is false	None of the practices are prohibited by Paul for the church (though he had ample opportunity to do so)	If practiced, the church should avoid legalism and sacramentalism

The observances do not SAVE YOU, thus they are not SACRAMENTAL	The observances do not SANCTIFY YOU, thus they are not observed out of OBEDIENCE

Notes

THE HISTORY OF SACRAMENTS AND ORDINANCES (BAPTISM)

BAPTISM				
Baptism is a Jewish ritual developed in the intertestamental period and closely related to repentance and restoration	Baptism was introduced into Scripture with John the Baptist, and was continued with the 12 Apostles among Jews	Baptism was performed in Ephesus and Corinth, apparently among Jews	Baptism was clearly separated from Paul's gospel. (1 Cor. 1:17)	Pauline epistles speak very little about baptism

Notes

THE HISTORY OF SACRAMENTS AND ORDINANCES (THE LORD'S SUPPER)

THE LORD'S SUPPER				
The "last supper" came to be known as the "Lord's Supper" (1 Cor. 11:20)	The early assemblies apparently partook of bread and wine as a memorial observance during worship gatherings	The Catholic church developed the doctrine of the Mass in which the elements of the "eucharist" become the body and blood of Jesus	The Protestants rejected the doctrine of the Mass in exchange for a doctrine of "spiritual presence"	The Anabaptists adopted a "memorial view" of the supper and observed it regularly in Christian worship

Notes

THE HISTORY OF SACRAMENTS AND ORDINANCES (OTHER ORDINANCES)

OTHER ORDINANCES	
NON-CATHOLIC	CATHOLIC
The ordinance of "foot washing" was adopted by Brethren groups	In addition to Baptism and Communion: Confirmation, Confession, Marriage, Holy Orders, Anointing of the Sick

Notes

A BRIEF HISTORY OF BAPTISM

<table>
<tr><th colspan="5">BAPTISM IN THE CHURCH TODAY</th></tr>
<tr><th>CATHOLIC VIEW</th><th>PROTESTANT VIEW</th><th>ANABAPTIST VIEW</th><th>EVANGELICAL VIEW</th><th>MID-ACTS VIEW</th></tr>
<tr><td>Baptism is Sacramental: an instrument of saving grace</td><td>The Protestant Reformation made baptism the sign and seal of the covenant, insisting on one and only one baptism as a requirement for church membership</td><td>The Anabaptists (and their spiritual kin) made baptism symbolic. Being martyred for it, they elevated it to greater practical importance than their theology expressed</td><td>Evangelicalism made baptism an "ordinance," thus mixing the sacramental and the symbolic into a requirement</td><td>The mid-Acts movement has rejected baptism altogether</td></tr>
<tr><td colspan="2">Administered officially only by the church</td><td>First administered by one another, then by the selected pastor</td><td>Traditionally administered by ordained clergy</td><td rowspan="2">Not administered</td></tr>
<tr><td colspan="2">Performed in the church during worship</td><td>Performed in small gatherings</td><td>Traditionally performed in the church during worship, but often in church-gatherings outside the church</td></tr>
<tr><th colspan="5">THEOLOGICAL SUPPORT GIVEN BY PROPONENTS OF EACH VIEW</th></tr>
<tr><td colspan="2">Baptism replaces circumcision and is thus required</td><td colspan="2">Baptism is viewed as wholly symbolic, even in Jewish days, and continues its symbolism. However, it is required for church membership</td><td>Baptism is viewed as wholly a Jewish required ritual, thus not applicable for the church age</td></tr>
</table>

Notes

THE BAPTISM OF JOHN, JESUS, AND YOU

WAS JOHN'S BAPTISM REALLY A BAPTISM OF WORKS?

Acts 18:24-28: Apollos, who had been preaching John's Baptism, was given a "more perfect" understanding of grace.	Acts 19:1-5: Those of Ephesus who had been baptized under John's baptism were rebaptized under grace.

THE BAPTISM OF JESUS

It was not an act of repentance	It was "to fulfill all righteousenss" (Matt. 3:15)	It was the ceremonial cleansing for the priestly role Jesus was about to fulfill	It previewed the testomony of God that will be heard at the inauguration of the Kingdom (Ps. 2)

BAPTISM TODAY

Is not a baptism of repentance	Is not a sacrament (as taught in Catholicism)
Is not a seal of the covenant (as taught in Reformed Theology)	Is a new baptism symbolic of the death, burial, and resurrection of our Lord

Notes

CHURCH LEADERSHIP: PRIEST OR PASTOR?

THE PRIESTHOOD				THE PASTORATE			
WHO HAS PRIESTS?	BIBLICAL BASIS	THEOLOGICAL ROLE	FUNCTIONAL ROLE	WHO HAS PASTORS?	BIBLICAL BASIS	THEOLOGICAL ROLE	FUNCTIONAL ROLE
Roman Catholic, Orthodox, Episcopalian	The priesthood in the Bible is fully Jewish, thus replacement theology is inherant in any Christian group that has a priest	Serves as an authoritative mediator between God and man and is the only authorized agent of the sacraments	Pastoral, receives confessions, allots church discipline, minor role in preaching and teaching	Protestants, Evangelicals, Fundamentalists	The teaching of elders, bishops, and pastors, used interchangably in the New Testament	Bible teaching and spiritual development	Pastoral, Bible teacher, spiritual mentor, church administrator

Notes

The CHURCH Graphically Presented

THE CHURCH LEADERSHIP: PASTOR OR ELDERS?

<table>
<tr><th colspan="2">Who has a pastor and who has elders?</th><th colspan="2">Does the Scripture call for multiple elders?</th><th>Is multiple eldership with a lead pastor biblical?</th><th>Does multiple eldership avoid problems?</th></tr>
<tr><td>Pastor</td><td>Elders</td><td>Arguments For</td><td>Arguments Against</td><td rowspan="2">There is no example in the Scripture of a "Lead Pastor" who is "first among equals" in an elder board, ruling a congregation</td><td rowspan="2">If churches of the New Testament had multiple elders, it did not avoid controversy, division, and sin in the congregation</td></tr>
<tr><td rowspan="3">Baptists, Calvary Chapel, Assembly of God, most independent churches</td><td rowspan="3">Bible churches, Presbyterian churches, most recent church starts</td><td rowspan="3">Scripture refers to elders of various locations in the plural</td><td rowspan="2">No names are given of two elders in a single church</td></tr>
<tr><td>Paul never wrote church-order issues to the elders (i.e.: Corinthians)</td><td>The modern churches with multiple elders have the same problems as those with a pastor</td></tr>
<tr><td>Qualifications are given in the singular, unlike for deacons</td><td>A "Lead Pastor" who is paid and runs daily operations is never "equal" among the elders</td><td>Multiple eldership puts members under spiritual authority of a small group of men who meet behind closed doors</td></tr>
</table>

Notes

HOW TO AVOID PROBLEMS IN THE CHURCH

HOW TO AVOID PROBLEMS IN THE CHURCH			
Make the Word of God the primary focus	Make every activity of the body transparent	Make the church a thinking organization rather than a goal-oriented organization	Make doctrinal parameters clear and upfront

Notes

HOW TO ADDRESS PROBLEMS IN THE CHURCH

HOW TO ADDRESS PROBLEMS IN THE CHURCH			
Make problems public as soon as possible	Make a decision on the problem as soon as possible	Love everyone on all sides of the problem	Get away from a program-driven mentality as soon as possible

Notes

DOES A CHURCH NEED A CREED OR CONFESSION?

DOES A CHURCH NEED A CREED OR CONFESSION?		
DEFINITIONS	DISCERNING WHICH IS WHICH	DO THEY WORK?
A Creed is Required for Membership	If everyone is required to sign it, it is a creed	Creeds become the focus rather than the Bible
A Confession is an official statement of doctrine used for church discipline	If everyone is subject to practice and teach it, it is a confession	Confessions cement error and become authoritative
A doctrinal statement is a description of the belief(s) of a church as a teaching parameter	If only teachers are required to use it for teaching paramaters, it is a doctrinal statement	Doctrinal statements clarify teaching for both teachers and students and create harmony
Creeds, confessions, and doctrinal statements are all written by men and not God and should be recognized as prone to error		

Notes

CREEDS OR CONFESSIONS: WHO USES WHAT?

CREEDAL GROUPS	CONFESSIONAL GROUPS	DOCTRINAL GROUPS
Catholics	Presbyterians - Westminster	Independent Fundamental Baptists
Orthodox	Methodists - Book of Discipline	Brethren Churches
Independent Fundamental Churches of America	Southern Baptist Convention	Bible Churches
General Association of Regular Baptist Churches		

Notes

IS HYPER-DISPENSATIONALISM HERESY?

WHAT A HYPER DISPENSATIONALIST WILL NOT DO	IS THIS HERESY?
Will not apply the teachings of Jesus directly to the church	Most evangelicals recognize that the Gospels were under the Law and will "somewhat" divide the word
	No essential teaching is based on a few words of Jesus
Will typically not perform water baptism	No evangelical will say that baptism is required for salvation
Might not observe the Lord's Supper	Evangelical churches often observe the Lord's Supper only 3-4 times per year, some less, and all say it is symbolic and optional
Teach repentance as a requirement for faith	Evangelical churches hold to the reformed doctrine of "Sola Fide" and often preach repentance but mean "change mind and be ready to change behavior."
Conclusion: ultra and hyper dispensationalism should be accepted or rejected on its Biblical argument, just like dispensationalism in general, and not dismissed as heresy	

Notes

www.ingramcontent.com/pod-product-compliance
Ingram Content Group UK Ltd.
Pitfield, Milton Keynes, MK11 3LW, UK
UKRC031012310726
14089UKWH00015B/254

* 9 7 8 1 9 4 5 7 7 4 3 6 2 *